The Essence of Twelve Step Recovery

"Damian McElrath is a born teacher; he presents complicated and difficult content in a clear and simple fashion. Thank you, Damian, for writing this book! It is a gift to all who are in search of the meaning of life."

—GAIL GLEASON MILGRAM, ED.D.

Professor/Director, Education and Training Division,
Rutgers University Center of Alcohol Studies

"Damian McElrath, a man with much integrity, has put together a simple but profound guide for addicts that goes to the very heart of what is needed for recovery. *The Essence of Twelve Step Recovery* has purpose and meaning beyond its pages. It's a must read for those looking to embrace or deepen their recovery."

—CRAIG NAKKEN, M.S.W.

Author of The Addictive Personality

"A terrific book! Damian McElrath has wonderfully captured the heartfelt journey that all of us in recovery must make, from the isolation and despair of addiction to the deeper connection to God, community, and a life of meaning and purpose."

—JOHN CURTISS

President, The Retreat

"Addiction may be a brain illness, but living with it requires (to paraphrase Jung) a spiritual upheaval. I have such a great respect for the fragility of the wounded heart ever-so-slightly opening to the idea of not being alone, not being afraid, not being on the outside, letting someone IN. As Damian McElrath so aptly puts it, few church services or rituals are equipped to penetrate the walls so many of us build. Yet, time after time, I have, just as Damian has, observed the most hardened soul within hours of being on a treatment unit drape his arms around the shoulders or hold the hand of another addict at the end of a group meeting, mouthing the words of a prayer they aren't sure they "get." I am certain that *The Essence of Twelve Step Recovery* will help those who come close enough in their journey to reach for it—which I believe will be many."

—MIKE SCHIKS, M.S., ACATA

Executive Director/CEO, Project Turnabout Addiction Recovery Center

The Essence of Twelve Step Recovery

Take It to Heart

Damian McElrath

Foreword by Richard Solly

Hazelden

Hazelden

Center City, Minnesota 55012

hazelden.org

ISBN: 978-1-59285-693-0

Editor's note

The names, details, and circumstances may have been changed to protect the privacy of those mentioned in this publication.

Alcoholics Anonymous, AA, and the Big Book are registered trademarks of Alcoholics Anonymous World Services, Inc.

12 11 10 09 08 6 5 4 3 2 1

Cover design by David Spohn

Interior design by David Swanson

Typesetting by David Swanson

To Sandy,
loving wife and gentle critic

Contents

From the Author

This book, *The Essence of Twelve Step Recovery*, is based on a series of four presentations that I developed for the patients of Jellinek, the long-term treatment unit at Hazelden, an alcohol and drug rehabilitation center located in Minnesota. The positive responses I received from patients about these lectures appeared genuine so I decided to write out my thoughts for myself, for the patients, and for anyone interested in getting an initial handle on AA spirituality in its *relational dimension*. However, my disclaimer is this: I am not an expert on spirituality.

Many definitions and descriptions of spirituality have emerged in the three decades since I began working in the world of recovery. However, it would be foolish for anyone to claim expertise in a matter that is so personal and subjective. I can only offer here my interpretation of "spiritual fitness" in an honest fashion. Moreover, my task is made easier by focusing on the spirituality of the Twelve Steps and the statement from the Big Book that I have quoted above: "The spiritual life is not a theory. *We have to live it.*"

Foreword

In *The Essence of Twelve Step Recovery*, Damian McElrath defines spirituality as "relational." That is, spirituality is not found alone in the desert, isolated on the snowy peak of a mountain top, or even in solitude on the shore of the Aegean Sea, but surprisingly, it can be found at home in our relationships with each other. This view of spirituality is an unusual one to come across today in our American culture of wanderlust, self-sufficiency, and independence.

McElrath believes that the spiritual path is best understood in the context of "the world of dialogue" with others. He even views the deeper Self as an a priori relationship, the first relationship upon which others are built, which in recovery we can develop or not. In fact, McElrath defines a triad of key relationships: self, others, and a Higher Power. These relationships create our spiritual center or "ultimate concern"; and as theologian Paul Tillich says in his book *The Meaning of Existence*, it is "the loss of a spiritual center" that arouses anxiety and meaninglessness, which are so characteristic of addiction.

Not surprisingly then, McElrath, a spiritual care provider for addicts and alcoholics, defines "the essential character of addiction" as "anti-relational," an isolation of intense magnitude that prohibits any kind of deep relationship. Disconnected from everything, everyone, and every place, the addicted person has truly lost his or her home—an inner landscape and fundamental relationship to the community that otherwise could normally help, nourish, and sustain a person. As a result, the chemically dependent person tumbles into an abyss of egotism or "a world of monologue" where only his or her voice, opinions, decisions, and wants matter. The alcoholic has no communication with anyone other than with his or her own obsessive need for intoxication; itself like a "voice," it is the only one the addict listens to. Cut off from the deeper self, the addict's only relationship is with an object: his or her drug.

I especially appreciate the author's all-inclusive definition of relationships. Whomever we meet, wherever we are, we are in a world of dialogue with others on our spiritual path. Spirituality is defined, McElrath says, by our ability to connect to a Higher Power through this community. To further emphasize its importance, the author draws our attention to the first word in the Twelve Steps: *We.*

The most critical community for the person in recovery is the fellowship of Alcoholics Anonymous or Narcotics Anonymous. There he or she first learns (or re-learns) that others bring, not hell as existentialist philosopher Jean-Paul Sartre believed, but help. Here, with others in the fellowship, the recovering person shares his or her experiences, strengths, and hopes. The stories told by others in the group help the recovering person learn that he or she too has a story to share, and in its telling lies the healing.

McElrath makes clear that abstinence alone is not spirituality; and spirituality isn't easy to come by. Most often, he says, the addict goes kicking and screaming to the death of his or her old intoxicated self, and only later, through some intervention, experiences "a rising (discovery) of the true self"—one of the three critical relationships. This discovery is a "spiritual awakening" that is achieved, sometimes dramatically and sometimes slowly, through education. In either case, what McElrath describes as a falling then a rising reminds me of the words of Nobel Prize poet Czeslaw Milosz, who writes in his poem "On Prayer" that in crisis sometimes a "reversal" happens, and what takes us down, what takes an addict down, can mysteriously reverse and now lift us up, "where everything is just the opposite and the word 'is' unveils a meaning we hardly envisioned." The meaning may be the very restoration of the fallen back from isolation into the healing world of others.

Of course, the resulting gratitude an alcoholic and addict can feel for this reversal or discovery is important. So much so that McElrath quotes Meister Eckhart, reminding us that if we say only one prayer in our lives, it should be "Thank you." However, I would argue that the addict really needs two prayers, the other one just as simple as the first: "Help me."

The author discusses how his triad of relationships (self, others, and Higher Power) is the key to understanding the Twelve Steps. In Step One, by admitting defeat, we find ourselves (or the self). In finding ourselves, we find the path back to others. And in this community or fellowship of others we find our Higher Power. In this way, the Twelve Steps help the recovering person heal all three main relationships at once.

The author's reference to Chardin that we are "spiritual beings having a human experience" emphasizes our relationships and being-in-the-world as truly the treasures of recovery. In the dependence on alcohol or drugs, relationships to others are buried, but sobriety unearths them. But how do we begin this spiritual journey forward into the new sobering light and life in our communities? To start is simple, says the author. Besides abstinence, all that is required is "a change of heart." And isn't *that* the essence of Twelve Step recovery?

Richard Solly

Author, *From Where the Rivers Come*

Introduction

In November 1977, I was completing my last quarter of a year-long internship in clinical pastoral education at Hazelden. I was a Franciscan priest at the time and had been for twenty-five years. The goal of this educational program was to remove clergy (of all denominations) from the classroom and their classical education and put them into contact with people in a variety of pastoral situations. This relational approach allowed the clergy to hone their personal skills and natural ability by processing their interactions with people in clinical pastoral situations. Individual sessions with a supervisor, and group settings that included both a supervisor and other students, allowed the clerical students to discover, as we used to joke, whether the patients had survived their spiritual encounter with us.

Our final analysis was to determine whether the spirit or our own ego was working within us; whether we had the best interests of the patient at heart or (unknown to us) our own vested interests; and whether it was the patient's feelings that counted or our own. Although I did not realize it at the time, this year-long internship was the most difficult and, at the same time, the most important year of my life. I was forty-eight years old, I had been a Franciscan priest for twenty-five years, and I was an educator and writer of some standing. As the internship came to its conclusion, I made a decision that changed the course of my life but left me hanging in limbo for a number of rocky years: I decided to leave the priesthood.

The decision to leave the priesthood meant that I would have to surrender my pastoral care duties, which in turn signified the end of my work as a chaplain on the rehabilitation unit (now called a recovery unit) at Hazelden. The unit I was working with when I made the decision was Jellinek (named after E. M. Jellinek, a psychiatrist who completed major research with alcoholics and after whom the Jellinek chart—which identifies the various stages of alcoholism—is named). Jellinek is the extended care unit, where patients who have been severely debilitated mentally, physically, and spiritually in their struggle with alcohol and chemicals and who need more time are placed. It was very painful for me to end my relationship with Jellinek. I had fallen in love with the setting, with the staff, and most of all with the patients.

After leaving the priesthood, I remained at Hazelden where I worked in a variety of positions. I was semi-retired when Hazelden invited me to become the chaplain on Jellinek in 2003. This was not the first time that things had come full circle in my life, but I believe that returning to Jellinek was a circle within the circumference of which I intimately and exclusively experienced the "digitus Dei" (finger of God). I think of Jellinek as a spiritual space as well as a place where spiritual growth is carefully nurtured. My role with the patients is to help them discover and remain spiritually centered. In this mutual encounter, their shared experiences in turn keep me spiritually centered.

It is with some hesitation that I undertake the task of writing this book. Having surrendered the priestly persona and descended from the priestly pedestal (both of my own choice), I hesitate making any pronouncements about spirituality. Additionally, there is a profound simplicity about AA spirituality, and in the past it has not been my nature to keep things simple. Let's just say that I have seen spirituality practiced and work in the lives of many recovering people as their journeys have unfolded on Jellinek. Perhaps I can risk describing it. The events of life do indeed come full circle. Much of what is of value and that which I have learned about spirituality before coming to Hazelden finds its completion in the community/fellowship of AA and in the practice of its Steps. So this is written in gratitude to the Jellinek patients, whose lives, struggles, and pain are witness to what spirituality is all about.

The examples of recovery that are portrayed in the following pages are composites of the many people I have encountered over the past twenty-five years. My gratitude extends to all the peers whose descents into and ascents from the "belly of the whale" have inspired and taught me much.

What follows is what I like to call the "spiritual protocols for recovery." They are: community/fellowship, which I discuss in chapter 1; the addictive process—its spiritual nature, discussed in chapter 2; the Twelve Steps—relational recovery, discussed in chapter 3; and the benchmarks of spiritual growth, discussed in chapter 4. In the book's conclusion I discuss the question: What, then, is spirituality?

"Be patient toward all that is unsolved in your heart and try to love the questions themselves . . ."

RAINER MARIA RILKE

CHAPTER 1

The Community

A Spiritual Protocol

The founders of Hazelden laid out the charter for its spirituality in the four simple expectations that its director composed for the guests coming for help:

1. Make your bed.

2. Be respectful of one another.

3. Attend the lectures on the Twelve Steps.

4. Talk to one another.

Rules 3 and 4 were the core principles of Hazelden's spirituality and have remained so for the past fifty-seven years (although at times it seems that one has to cut through multiple levels of other services to discover that they still remain the heart and focus of the treatment process). The process is not much different from that enacted by Dr. Bob and Bill W. when in 1935 they began sharing their experiences with one another. The two men took some basic spiritual principles from the Oxford movement to help the first one hundred AA members. Bill W. eventually crafted these principles into the Twelve Steps. The spiritual protocol was simple: "Talk to one another and follow these principles."

When I talk with the patients on Jellinek, either individually or in group, I emphasize the simplicity of the protocol for living a life free from alcohol and chemicals. Often I preface our discussion with a story about my thirty-nine-year-old stepson, Steve, who was the youngest person in the United States to be struck with a very lethal but extremely rare strain of cancer. The very knowledgeable oncologist who took his case and researched the treatments previously employed for this type of cancer discovered a very intensive course of treatment that would need to extend for six months. Many people not as young as Steve have been unable to complete the treatment because of its debilitating side effects. Fortunately, Steve was able to deal with the physical and mental strains and the cancer is now in remission. However, nothing will be the same, and there is no guarantee that the cancer will not return. But the doctor's message was simple: Follow this protocol and you will live. Half measures would have availed him nothing.

The same message is intended for those suffering from the disease of chemical dependency: "If you have decided you want what we have and are willing to go to any length to get it— then you are ready to take certain steps" (*Alcoholics Anonymous*, p. 58). Hazelden's protocol for recovery demands participation in a community/fellowship and the practice of the Twelve Steps. No matter how, over the years, Hazelden's recovery program has grown and its services multiplied, the essential protocol remains the same. "Rarely have we seen a person fail who has thoroughly followed our path" (*Alcoholics Anonymous*, p. 58). In other words: Do this and you shall live!

Hazelden's protocol responds to the fundamental yearnings of our human nature, the most important aspect of which is to be connected with other human beings—in other words, to be *relational*. One of the most insidious aspects of chemical dependency is that it is *anti-relational*. Isolation, self-absorption, and self-centeredness are the largest spiritual blocks. The most common wrong turn that the chemically dependent take on their journey is that which severs relationships with self, spouse, children, parents, friends, and the God of their understanding.

The Community

One of my favorite quotations (whose source I truthfully admit I cannot remember) is: "Our journey through life is a community affair; someone has to say: 'I will be with you.'" Other people are essential to our lives as human beings. This is even more true for those in recovery. That is the reason why recovery is often described as a "we" program. The community/fellowship, together with the Twelve Steps, make up the two essential elements of the protocol. The person seeking recovery must reconnect with his true self, with others, and with his Higher Power (the God of his understanding).

The truth that most of us fail to recognize is that each of us, staff members and peers alike, has a precious gift that we bring to the community of recovery. Most of us give little thought to the value of, as someone put it, our "life experiences, well digested." One need only remember the special encounter between Bill W. and Dr. Bob. When the two of them met and shared their life experiences "well digested," it was the beginning of the AA community. In the following quote, from "Doctor Bob's Nightmare" in the Big Book, Dr. Bob speaks about why his relationship with Bill W. was so important.

He gave me information about the subject of alcoholism which was undoubtedly helpful. Of far more importance was the fact that he was the first living human with whom I had ever talked, who knew what he was talking about in regard to alcoholism from actual experience. In other words, he talked my language. *He knew all the answers, and certainly not because he had picked them up in his reading* (Alcoholics Anonymous, *p. 180).*

The recovering community needs to be continually advised that within its ranks/fellowship there is a fountain of wisdom from the members' composite experiences with and without drugs and alcohol that they can share with one another and use to confront one another, to support one another, and to learn from one another. This total experience is a great gift that nurtures the entire community. Granted, even in the best of communities there are strains of pettiness, backbiting, disrespect, and intolerance. But even these negative qualities can become the fertilizer that enriches the soil and seed of the real community. However, in no way can this negative component of community offset the conventional wisdom of the members' well-digested experiences. No one can say that "there is nothing spiritual going on in their lives; telling their story to another human being is sacred ground."

The dynamic is the same for all the guests who arrive at Hazelden—the men and women from all walks of life, "from every shire's end," young and old, rich and poor, who populate the recovery units. Rabbi Saul Rubin is quoted as saying: "We have stories to tell, stories that provide wisdom about the journey of life. What more have we to give one another than our 'truth' about our human adventure as honestly and as openly as we know how?" After a short stay on the skilled medical unit where one's physical appropriateness is monitored, the newly arrived patient is immediately transferred to one of Hazelden's recovery units. One of Hazelden's major insights, taken from AA, has been that recovery takes place neither in isolation nor in consultation with experts but with "one alcoholic talking to another over a cup of coffee."

The first week on the unit is usually difficult for the patient: full of stress, anxiety, fear, anger, resentment, and a myriad of other thoughts and feelings. The guest builds all sorts of walls to protect herself and her vulnerabilities. But gradually things happen so that the newcomer slowly moves from the emotional position of "not belonging," of "not being accepted," to the experience that she is truly part of a community of like-sufferers. The discovery that one truly belongs is a genuinely welcome one.

John was from New York and had a history of cocaine use. Early on in his stay at Hazelden he had a very aggressive manner, partly due to his culture and his cocaine use, but mostly because of the fear that he experienced while being with a group of people who, for the most part, allowed themselves to be vulnerable, and, from his New York vantage point, allowed their weaknesses to be shown to other people. He felt that the best thing to do was to be aggressive and not let anybody in. Because he kept pushing people away with his gruff manner and unwillingness to share anything, most of his peers left him alone. John's roommate Jim, however, was relentless in urging John to open up and he did it in such a non-threatening manner that John began taking risks and sharing some things with Jim, then with others, and finally with the whole group. At his final community meeting before he departed, John had become the community leader and was encouraging the newcomers to open up and share. John just recently celebrated his tenth anniversary of recovery.

Is there an explanation for John's turnabout in the above story? Well, it is really very simple. From the very first day that the doors of Hazelden opened, it has created an environment that is safe and respectful of the worth and dignity of each individual crossing its threshold. The self-contained living units that have evolved for men and eventually women are sanctuaries where individuals, broken and ashamed, can share their experiences, their hopes, and their individual and communal strengths in a serene, nonthreatening setting, twenty-four hours a day, waking and sleeping. When a patient has trouble sleeping, he can always find someone awake with whom he can share his stories. "The stories that people tell have a way of taking care of them. If stories come to you, care for them. And learn to give them away where they are needed. Sometimes a person needs a story more than food to stay alive" (Lopez, p. 48).

As simple as it may seem, that is the special dynamic. In my conferences with patients, I use the ordinary example of my "speaking" to them. In talking to them I am presenting them with the *gift* of my knowledge—whatever I can bring to bear on the subject from my education, background, experience, and intuition. I tell them I am *gracing* them by my presence and participation in the dialogue. Conversely, I ask them what gift they are giving to me. There is usually a silence for they are not certain of the direction in which this is going. My suggestion is that they are *gracing* me with the gift of listening respectfully to what I am saying. Even beyond that, sometimes there is mutual sharing/dialogue and in that way we are *gracing/gifting* (grace as a gift of the God of our understanding) one another by sharing. Talking, listening, and sharing is the spiritual dynamic that inspires and builds up the community—all drawn from the model of the Fellowship of AA. (It should come as no surprise that the ability to be genuinely present and to listen attentively is the most important skill that counselors can bring to their sessions with patients.)

There is something redemptive and very spiritual about this process. It derives from the reality of a "healing" community and at the same time a personal acceptance of one's individual vulnerability or woundedness. Where two or three are gathered, the God of our understanding is present. In the AA Fellowship "everybody opens up about their brokenness and their failures, and they heal . . . What happens in Churches is just the opposite. . . . We sit there with our pain and brokenness, and we never share it and we don't heal. Our Churches are just the opposite of a healing community. . . . We will have to work hard toward becoming the kind of community where it is safe to tell your story." (Hilton, p. 58.)

Another example of this relational and communal spirituality rests in the choices that we make as human beings. Throughout the successive developmental stages of our lives, we can choose to *be with others* or to *go it alone*. A chemically dependent person, however, does not have that choice. Alcohol and chemicals force her to go it alone and ostracize her from the love and support of another/others. She chooses self-centeredness, isolation, self-absorption, and a non-relational spirituality. The Big Book characterizes such an individual as "self-will run riot." There is a community but it is me, myself, I, and my addiction.

DIAGRAM 1

World of Addiction =

WORLD OF MONOLOGUE

Addict is a prisoner in an iron bubble.
This is the world of the "I"

- *Chooses non-relatedness*
- *Self-centeredness • Isolation*

God speaking through others
cannot breach the bubble

GOD OF HIS UNDERSTANDING
HAS NO PORT OF ENTRY

DIAGRAM 2

World of Recovery =

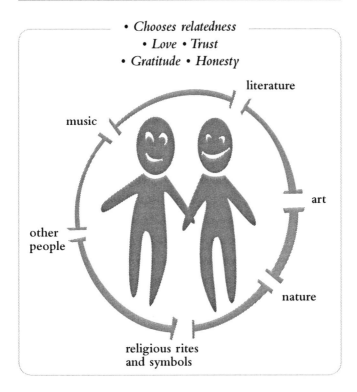

- *Chooses relatedness*
- *Love* • *Trust*
- *Gratitude* • *Honesty*

literature

music

art

other
people

nature

religious rites
and symbols

GOD OF HIS UNDERSTANDING
HAS MANY PORTS OF ENTRY—
ESPECIALLY OTHER PEOPLE

Losing contact with people and the community, she inevitably loses contact with the God of her understanding who is unable to break through the perimeter of her addiction.

As diagram 1 shows, the world that the addictive person inhabits is a self-enclosed, self-contained circle. The conversation that the addictive person thinks that she is having is surreal. In fact, it is nothing but a *world of monologue* as she is not listening to anyone else. The receptors of one's soul are sealed off from any real, serious engagement with another/others (family members, friends, recovering people). Even more serious is that the God of her understanding cannot pierce the iron bubble that the addict has constructed for herself, for when it comes to chemical dependency, God usually works through other people. A real spiritual awakening is realized only when one truly embraces the formula: "I cannot do it by myself; I need others to help me." In one sense this is the personality change envisioned in recovery.

In the recovery journey, shown in diagram 2, the addict is called upon to choose a relational spirituality, and in so doing she chooses a world of love, trust, and attention directed toward others. It is the world of open-mindedness, willingness, and honesty. Others are no longer outside the circumference but are now welcomed inside the perimeter. It is the *world of dialogue*. In fact this relational choice allows the God of her understanding to create channels into the spirit/soul of the addict through other people whom the addict has included in her circle. It is the beginning of the creation of a caring and healing community. It is the world of the "we" in contrast to the world of the "I" (ego).

It was so rewarding to see Paul come out of his shell, with great reluctance at first, and then hesitantly respond to the overtures of his peers who refused to let him retreat to his room or be by himself. When he first came into my office, it was like pulling teeth to get him to say anything at all. Silence was the shield that prevented him from getting wounded. What emerged slowly but surely as he began to understand the disease that controlled him, was a delightful person, slow to speak, but finally willing to speak as a member of his newly found community. And when he spoke, people listened. Paul is now in his eleventh year of recovery, an active member of the Fellowship, and a reliable sponsor to many.

A Fundamental Spiritual Principle

A very important quality contributing to recovery is that of trust. My formula is this: Trust demands that we take risks; any risk-taking leaves us open to the possibility of being hurt, in other words allowing a point of entry into our human vulnerability. My suggestion is that the conscious acknowledgement of this vulnerability is the foundation for one's spirituality. Indeed we are all imperfect human beings (recovering people are mindful of this more than most and the acceptance of this status works to their advantage more than most). Another way of putting it is that we are human beings lacking wholeness toward which each individual's life journey is directed. I paraphrase what Carl Jung wrote to Bill W.: At its root, alcoholism is a spiritual disease at the basis of which is man's yearning for wholeness.

We are vulnerable from the first moment we are born. In a sense, life is one continual strategy of keeping ourselves from being hurt/wounded. Every time it happens, we vow it won't happen again, and so we clothe ourselves with steel-plated armor to deflect the harsh rapiers of human meanness.

In Native American wisdom one can find the intimation that all brothers and sisters belong to the scarred clan. We all carry wounds that we have suffered as children, adolescents, and adults in the morning stage of our lives. The medicinal hope for all of us is that instead of withdrawing and licking our wounds, we will have dealt with them bravely and courageously, thereby allowing the wounds to heal from within so that, even though the scars remain, there is no longer an infection. In the afternoon of our lives, the scars in turn serve as a medicinal shield letting people know that they are now dealing with a person of strength and courage. Our wounds now attest to our status as "wounded healers."

Jenny had been through treatment multiple times. She had lost her children, her husband, and all her friends except for one who refused to abandon her. Jenny's friend continued to call her despite the fact that most of the time she found herself on the end of an answering machine. At Hazelden, Jenny would remain in her room until she was put on room restriction. Jenny continued to isolate herself until one day at a full-group session, her peers and the staff members came up to her one by one and each told her one quality they admired in her and then hugged her. Jenny cried and cried. It was the breakthrough. Slowly but surely Jenny accepted her vulnerability, took risks, began to take little steps of trust, and emerged from her isolative shell. She has recovered her children, who told her that it was so good to have their real mother back. A "wounded healer," Jenny is now a very active participant in the Fellowship.

A Healing Community

Essentially, the community of recovery is a healing community, the core component of which is dialogue. There are two parts to spirituality. The first part is the mystery, which does not at all reside in the God of our understanding but in the God who is beyond all understanding. The second part is the human. A theme that permeates the writings of Thomas Merton, a renowned twentieth century author, is that to be truly human is to be truly spiritual, and to be truly spiritual is to be truly human. It is the human part that allows us entry into the visible realm of spirituality. It is the visible universe that contains and manifests the signs of an invisible presence—the "cloud of the unknowing." We have spent time wrestling with this in suggesting previously that the God of one's understanding can and in reality does intimate his workings/presence through men and women in the Fellowship, the clearest evidence of a Higher Power. But there are other visible signs of this invisible presence that speak to us and our restlessness: music, literature, the splendor of the universe, the animal world, and religious rites and rituals—a mixed ensemble of voices that resonate with something deep within us. This may be difficult to accept/understand for those whose perception of reality does not reach beyond the visible. However, it is definitely embedded in the origins and history of the AA movement with its appeal to a God of one's understanding. It not only encourages us to go deeper, but to accept the visible and look beyond it to see if we can match the "restlessness" of what is "deep within" with the "rest and quietude" that is "beyond."

"It may be that when we no longer know what to do, we have come to our real work, and when we no longer know which way to go, we have begun our real journey."

WENDELL BERRY

CHAPTER 2

The Spirituality of Addiction

Our Encounter with Crises

Is there really something spiritual about the addictive process? Recovery—perhaps. But addiction—no! On the other hand, since the addictive process ultimately covets a person's spirit, there is value in scrutinizing the price that people are willing to pay to capture a wholeness no matter how fleeting or deceiving.

Let us recall our journey once again. Even though each person's journey is unique and the spiritual path has many detours, dead ends, and wrong turns, everyone's journey has a pattern of interruptions that have the potential for growth or regression. I refer to those interruptions as crises or (as William Bridges titles his book) transitions.

These crises interrupt the normal ebb and flow of our lives with unexpected riptides. Crises are times of ambiguity, times of decision, and even sacred moments. There is a negative element to the crisis, characterized by disorientation, a loss of identity, disengagement, and disenchantment, and caused by any number of events: the death of one's spouse, boredom with one's job, divorce, or the empty nest syndrome. At the nadir, or low point, of the crisis, the individual, figuratively speaking, finds himself, like Jonah, in the belly of the whale. This serves as a fitting spiritual metaphor for the darkness and silence in which the soul finds itself, in a prison that appears to allow for no escape. The pain associated with waiting and having no knowledge of the outcome can be excruciating. Our decision is either to reject the challenge of change by returning to what is known, comfortable, and risk-free, or to accept the invitation to a new beginning. The crisis is telling us that one stage of our life is over and done with. To return to it would be safe but spiritually atrophying. To accept the new beginning demands risk and courage and opens the gate to the unknown. It is at this point that many addicts falter. To leave the comfort and bosom of the addictive siren is too much to ask. There has to be an easier way.

My own life offers a clear example of the stages of crisis. In 1976 I came to Minnesota to participate in a year-long clinical pastoral education program at Hazelden. During that time I fell in love. Failing to live the celibate life that I had vowed and unwilling to lead a double life, I made the decision to leave the priesthood. I decided to end a way of life that I had embraced for over twenty-five years. It was a crisis of the utmost severity. I was truly in the belly of the whale, tossed about by painfully mixed emotions including the bile of indigestible shame and guilt. Living in such abandonment and uncertainty was too much, so I resolved the crisis by returning to the priesthood, to the safety and security of what was known and safe. I was like a person crossing a suspension bridge: once the swaying started, panic set in and I thought it best to retreat to the starting point.

But this is not the end of the story. Some years later I went through this same process again. This time I did have the resolve and strength to leave my entrenched way of life, embrace the unknown, accept the love that was offered to me, and leave a life of celibacy for one of intimacy.

Someone has written that every crisis, every descending/ascending spiral that we endure is an encounter with our mortality. Unless we have respect for and learn from these crises, we will go kicking and screaming into death. Still, it is important that we view a crisis as a normal part of our spiritual journey and growth—a situation that demands of us internal change.

Angeles Arrien, in *The Second Half of Life*, has described the spiral in the following fashion:

The descent into darkness—the unknown or undeveloped aspect of our nature—and the ascent into greater awareness, authenticity and faith, lead us to a discovery of our essential self beyond ego and personal desire. In both directions we encounter our shadows, the unclaimed, undesired and unbefriended aspects of our nature. To become fully developed human beings, we must confront our demons and our angels. If we can do this successfully, we free ourselves from the illusion of who we think we are. We are delivered into the mystery of our true, essential being, and are able to generate a new domain of freedom, that is anchored in wisdom, love and faith (p. 13).

The process of addiction and recovery is a mortal crisis in every sense of the word. Applying the aforementioned image of a descending/ascending spiral will help put addiction in the context of everyone's life journey, since it is a universal human experience revealing the "heavens and hells" that our nature seeks desperately to conceal.

The Addictive Self

In this discussion of the spirituality of addiction, it will help to have some understanding of what the downward spiral of the addictive process is all about. I think an excellent, and indeed the clearest, description can be found in the book *The Addictive Personality* by Craig Nakken, a book that I would recommend to anyone searching for an existential analysis of the disease of addiction.

He describes an addiction as a pathological relationship of love and trust with an object or event rather than with oneself, another, others, or one's Higher Power. The essential character of addiction is that it is non-relational and therefore non-spiritual, no matter how jealous and zealous the addict is in defending his mood change or high as a spiritual experience. It relies upon the duality of selves that compose our human natures. The literature of the Western world, from Paul of Tarsus to Carl Jung, recognizes the presence of man's duality—that there is another self inside of us waiting to exploit and control the lives of every one of us.

Carl Jung said it best when he commented that "what drives people to war within themselves is the intuition or knowledge that they consist of two people in opposition to one another" (p. 173). Applied to the process of addiction and recovery, our false self uses the chemical to drug our true self (internal change—the first step in the downward spiral), to rob us of our relationship with others (lifestyle change—the second step in the downward spiral), and to smother the spirit within (life-breakdown stage—the final step in the downward spiral). This whole process, as shown in diagram 3, is simply another frightening reflection of the eternal struggle between the two selves that dwell within us.

The Descending/Ascending Spiral

In the downward spiral, the addictive self compels us against our will to substitute that which is most important to us as human beings—intimacy with another/others—for intensity with a chemical. There is a terrifying disconnect from reality as over the course of the addictive journey the individual moves from the land of the living to the land of objects. No matter how hard one may try, one cannot have intimacy with an object. It is difficult to breathe when one's spirit is being crushed from within.

Associated with the loss of these relationships, which diagram 3 portrays, is a negative value system, which the addictive self automatically evokes to keep others at a distance and one's true self in chains. As described in the Big Book, these negative values include self-centeredness, fear, dishonesty, and resentments, which serve as formidable barriers to the relationships that are part and parcel of what makes us human.

The bottom of the spiral (remembering that each one's nadir is different) is a place, sacred or unholy, where one loathes being, where one experiences one's personal hell together with its demons. The disconnectedness and feeling of "relational" abandonment becomes so complete, the pain so unrelenting,

DIAGRAM 3

The Addictive Spiral

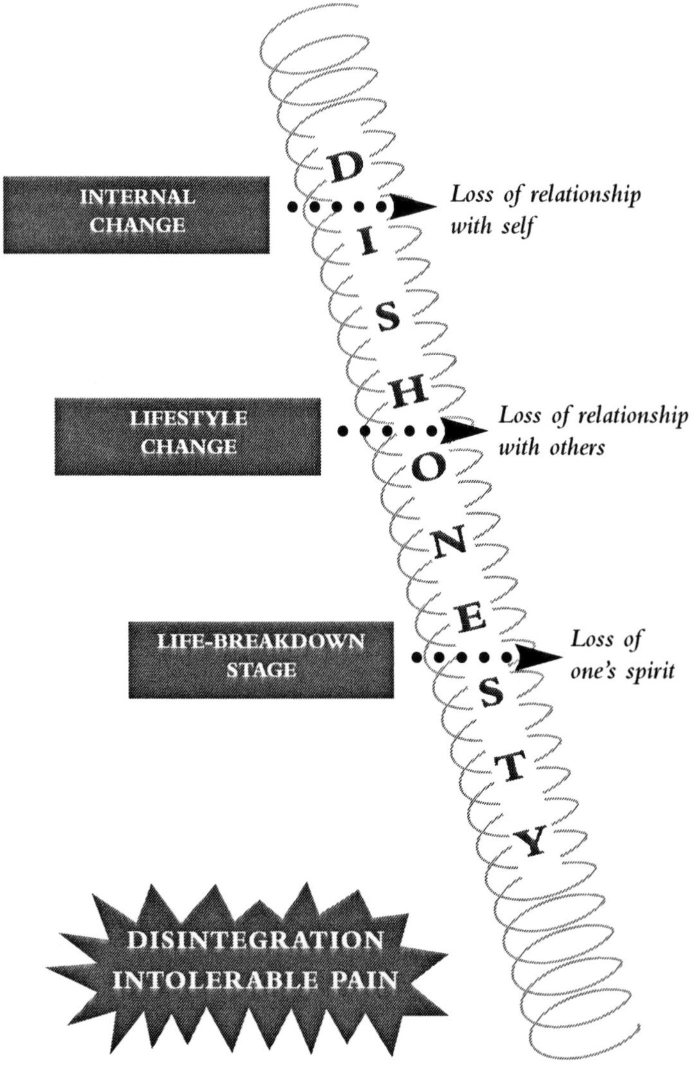

INTERNAL CHANGE	Loss of relationship with self
LIFESTYLE CHANGE	Loss of relationship with others
LIFE-BREAKDOWN STAGE	Loss of one's spirit

DISHONESTY

DISINTEGRATION
INTOLERABLE PAIN

the hopelessness so unremitting, that the addict feels that he is dying. The addiction keeps up and intensifies the pressure so that the addict will do anything to lessen the pain, push back the tide of despair, relieve the loneliness and hopelessness, and absolve himself of the shame and guilt. More drugs provide only a momentary relief. The loss of the spirit is so pronounced that suddenly there is the whisper from our demons that life is no longer worth living.

It is at the bottom of the spiral that the addict truly feels his woundedness, the full power of the other self. At the bottom is the pain, coupled with the sense of unknowing and despair. Left to himself, the addict may simply be content with licking his wounds. But licking won't do. The wounds have to heal from the inside out, even if it means leaving scars.

> Michelle's life affords a clear example of the downward spiral. A forty-five-year-old mother of four, she appears to have crossed the line when she began hiding the liquor to quiet the nagging of her husband. She sensed that something was happening when she promised herself that she would only have one drink in the afternoon before her husband came home from work, and quickly found that one was never sufficient. Things got worse when she began to pass out on the couch and couldn't prepare supper for the family. As her life became more unmanageable, she no longer cared what people thought or that her children avoided her and no longer brought their friends home to visit. Meals were unpleasant experiences and worse when Michelle passed out at the table. Her life was breaking down; she was filled with a free-floating anxiety and would cry for no reason at all. She felt as though her spirit were dying within her. Michelle, because of the addictive self, had lost the relationships that were most important to her: the relationships with her real self, with others, and with the God of her understanding.
>
> Michelle's family sponsored an intervention. Michelle went for treatment, but refused the recommendation for extended

DIAGRAM 4

The Relational Spiral

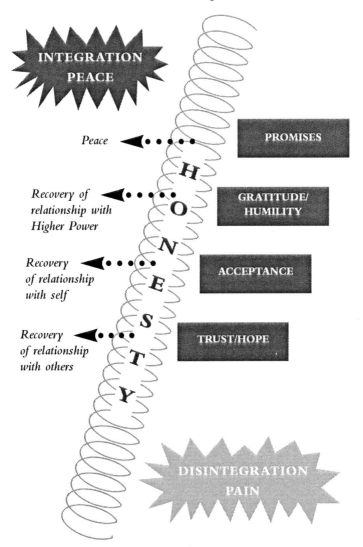

care on the grounds that her children needed her. The children were grateful to have their "real mother" back, not her addictive self. But Michelle relapsed and died the following Christmas from complications due to her resumption of drinking. The person who Michelle truly was had been overcome by the seductive sirens of alcohol.

In the vast majority of cases, addicts are not totally abandoned. The potential for recovery is always there. Certainly, the God of a person's understanding will not abandon that person. Even though an addict may realize that she can descend no further, family members and friends continue to extend their love. An addict may stumble upon someone who is in the Fellowship, or a member of that community may be led to seek out the addict.

When an addict discovers that her own strength and efforts have been to no avail, this leads to another discovery: that the strength of others is sufficient for her. Trusting in that strength, the addict begins to heal/mend through the redemptive power of others, reflecting the slow but certain recognition of a Higher Power in the collective strength of a community that has gone through the same descending/ascending journey.

If the addict continues to lick her wounds, she will come away spiritually empty and will not experience what is commonly referred to as "ego deflation" at depth. But real transformation occurs with the hand of the helpless one reaching out to grasp the hand of the helper—the beginning of the spiritual awakening. It is the humble acknowledgement that "I cannot do it by myself; I need others to help me." It is the gradual recovery of one's lost "relational" spirituality.

It can be looked upon as a redisplay of the majestic painting in the Sistine Chapel in Rome where Michelangelo portrayed the finger of God reaching down to touch the finger of Adam. With that gesture, God graced Adam with the gift of life. In a similar fashion, one alcoholic reaches out to another with the gift of sobriety—the experience of the "we" program.

No matter what the nature or explanation of this seminal experience/awakening, it is the beginning of the ascent, the upward part of the spiral that witnesses the re-establishment of relationships and the cultivation of the positive moral qualities that are the glue cementing these relationships: trust, gratitude, acceptance, and honesty.

Instrumental and fundamental to this reconstruction process is the quality of trust—trusting others in the Fellowship. It is imperative that we listen to others who have experienced recovery rather than trust ourselves. For in early recovery it is not easy to discern which of our selves—the essential or false self, our angel or demon—is whispering to us. Our demons are slick and can simulate our angels quite effortlessly.

Allow me to quote once again from one of my favorite spiritual authors, Angeles Arrien:

> *The raw experience of descent (descending into our own inner terrain and expelling all that is false and at odds with our essential being) prepares the way for the increased self-knowledge and self-acceptance that are honest and true, anchored in a kind of self-confidence that is neither inflated nor deflated. The descent allows us to experience the ascent with genuine hopefulness, curiosity and an ennobled spirit. If we have done the rigorous work of descending to face our false self, we may then ascend to experience the joy of our essential self without pretense or judgment (pp. 63–64).*

In this quote Arrien is describing a dying/rising process comparable to the dying/rising process at work in recovery—a dying of the addictive self and a rising (discovery) of the true self.

"If the only prayer you say in your whole life is 'Thank you,'
that would suffice."

MEISTER ECKHART

CHAPTER 3

The Twelve Steps: Relational Spirituality

Prior to the composition of the Twelve Steps by Bill W. in 1939, AA was already represented by one hundred recovering people talking to one another and, together with their hopes and strengths, sharing their "personal experiences, well digested." This was, indeed, the spirituality of relationships. The earliest example of this "personal experience, well-digested" in the AA movement comes from the mouth of Dr. Bob himself. It is worth repeating: "He [Bill W.] gave me information about the subject of alcoholism which was undoubtedly helpful. *Of far more importance was the fact that he was the first living human with whom I had ever talked, who knew what he was talking about in regard to alcoholism from actual experience. In other words, he talked my language"* (*Alcoholics Anonymous,* p. 180).

Four years after Bill W. and Dr. Bob first talked and shared their experiences, Bill W. composed the Twelve Steps. It is important to recognize that the basic Steps were rooted in the religious practices of the Oxford Group to which Bill initially belonged. The Oxford Group was an evangelical Christian movement that sought to restore the sense of community and simplicity as the group imagined it existing in early Christianity. Bill's first version of the Steps included only six Steps, which were directed to the threefold relationship about which we have been dealing: self, others, and God. So that there would be no misunderstanding, no "wiggly room," Bill expanded the six Steps to twelve and offered them as "suggestions" for those who wished to lead a life free from alcohol.

The references to God in the Steps offended the agnostics and atheists among the first one hundred members, so Bill compromised by using the words "Power greater than ouselves" in the Second Step, and the words "God as we understood Him" in the Third and Eleventh Steps. Bill decided to leave "God" in Steps Five and Six, allowing the "conscientious objectors" to wrestle with their own angels and inherited biases. In so doing, he recognized the right and tendency of recovering people to grumble about things just like the rest of the human race. And it has been so ever since.

The Twelve Steps focus on our connectedness with self, others, and a God of our understanding. The following, then, is my personal interpretation of the power of the Twelve Steps to bring about recovery through the restoration and reconstruction of the threefold relationship that gives meaning to our lives.

A Circular View of the Steps

In diagram 5, I have sorted the Steps into circles and arranged them into three groups. Circles represent continuity, protection, strength, and completeness, and they seemed an appropriate way to express our relationships with self, others, and a Higher Power supported and enhanced by the qualities just listed. Moreover, the Steps divide themselves comfortably into three distinct triads.

The following pages are not intended as a substitution for *Twelve Steps and Twelve Traditions,* but simply as a supplemental commentary. I make no pretense of being the final spokesperson, much less authority, for the meaning of recovery or the Twelve Steps. However, I think it important at the outset to remember that the Steps/spiritual principles (a "simple kit of spiritual tools laid at our feet," [*Alcoholics Anonymous,* p. 25]), are intended to be "guides (direction or suggestions) to spiritual progress." In other words, they are not steps in a ladder that have to be ascended one after the other. Its not as if a person needs to "get" Steps One and Two or Three before practicing Step Eleven. Likewise, Step Nine does not have to be implemented before putting Step Ten into practice. Quite the contrary, these spiritual principles will capture a person's heart (and be internalized) at different stages of the individual's spiritual journey.

> **Step One:** We admitted we were powerless over alcohol—that our lives had become unmanageable.

DIAGRAM 5

The Twelve Steps

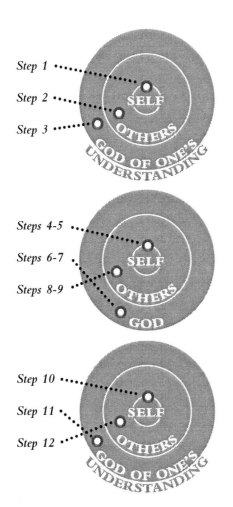

Step 1 ·······
Step 2 ·······
Step 3 ·······

SELF
OTHERS
GOD OF ONE'S UNDERSTANDING

Steps 4-5 ·······
Steps 6-7 ·······
Steps 8-9 ·······

SELF
OTHERS
GOD

Step 10 ·······
Step 11 ·······
Step 12 ·······

SELF
OTHERS
GOD OF ONE'S UNDERSTANDING

The quality of our relationship with the God of our understanding is absolutely contingent upon the quality of our own relationship with others.

> **Step Two:** Came to believe that a Power greater than ourselves could restore us to sanity.

> **Step Three:** Made a decision to turn our will and our lives over to the care of God *as we understood Him.*

Step One deals with self and the admission of one's powerlessness over chemicals. It is the Step by which individuals acknowledge their woundedness and imperfection, and serves to open the gate to the discovery of one's true self. This is the small, innermost circle on the chart.

Step Two can be positioned in the context of reconnecting with others, the Fellowship. For many, in the beginning of their recovery, other human beings were positioned as the Higher Power through which the God of their understanding would be speaking when it came to the disease of chemical dependency. The Second Step helps to establish relationships essential to recovery and accounts for the middle circle in the diagram. It reflects the truth of the quotation that I mentioned previously: "Our journey through life is a community affair; someone has to say 'I will be with you.'"

Step Three is depicted by the outer circle that encloses the other two. This Step puts the God of our understanding into the equation and is probably, together with Step One, the most challenging of the Steps—just as challenging as the formidable expectation of total surrender in the Judaic-Christian tradition. (My own personal belief is that Steps Two and Three do not receive enough attention in treatment programs. As a result, patients are short-changed and relapses are more likely to occur.)

The first three Steps serve as the foundation for the spiritual edifice. Acceptance of one's powerlessness (surrender to the disease) is central to recovery. A transfer of power is necessary: from admission to acceptance of powerlessness, from compliance (external—going through the motions) to acceptance (internal—unconditional surrender) of the power that this disease of chemical dependency has over us. As the recovering person has been told over and over again: The foundation for the disease has been cemented by the brick and mortar of a mental obsession (that I can *control* my drinking) and a physical compulsion that can only be removed by the jackhammer of surrender.

Once the old mortar has been carefully and painfully removed piece by piece (Step One), then the concrete of a Power greater than oneself can be poured into the mold of a new foundation that relies not on an inflated ego but upon the power of others/another (Second and Third Steps). These Steps are the commencement of a new life—the initial reconnection with self, others, and a God of our understanding.

Step Three is a daunting suggestion. A simple way to approach it is to take small steps. Since in the past we admit that it was the height of insanity and absurdity that we turned our lives and wills over to the care and management of a chemical, we can start by turning the management of the chemical over to God's direction. Turning over our lives and wills should be easy, but, given our self will, it is not. In the last analysis it all starts with willingness—the key to this Step. Translated into practical terms, "made a decision" simply means that we can either choose recovery or choose relapse. If we choose recovery, then we must act accordingly by using the "recovery capital" put at our disposal, namely: the Twelve Steps (especially Steps Ten through Twelve), a sponsor, the Big Book, meetings, and the faithful execution of service. We know that we initiate the acceptance of Step Three when we have undertaken the daily practice of Steps Four through Twelve and thereby make a daily conscious choice for recovery over relapse.

And so it plays out with the remainder of the Steps. We are invited to deal with the circles of relationships through a series of spiritual exercises (Steps Four through Twelve), a group of practices meant to nurture the commitments that we have made in Steps One through Three, which in synoptic fashion have presented the problem (powerlessness) and the solution (a power greater than ourselves).

Step Four: Made a searching and fearless moral inventory of ourselves.

Step Five: Admitted to God, to ourselves, and to another human being the exact nature of our wrongs.

Step Six: Were entirely ready to have God remove all these defects of character.

Step Seven: Humbly asked Him to remove our shortcomings.

Step Eight: Made a list of all persons we had harmed, and became willing to make amends to them all.

Step Nine: Made direct amends to such people wherever possible, except when to do so would injure them or others.

Steps Four and Five, the inmost circle, urge us to take a long, hard, and penetrating look at ourselves and our lives up to this point, at the exact nature of our wrongs, and to expose the wounds, large or small, that were inflicted by the addiction and require healing.

This inventory helps us to focus on those relationships where our behavior has wounded others. The middle circle, which reflects Steps Eight and Nine, then invites us to offer the balm of amends intended to heal from the inside out. It is interesting to note that "if we are painstaking" in the fulfillment of these two Steps, we will "know a new freedom and a new happiness," accept a complete set of promises, and realize "that

God is doing for us what we could not do for ourselves" (*Alcoholics Anonymous,* pp. 83–84).

The outer circle represented by Steps Six and Seven reminds us to invite God once again into the healing process. In some respects these are the most challenging of all the Steps. "Entirely ready" and "humbly asked" hardly allow for any wiggle room. They reinforce the demand for surrender and humility. It is interesting that these two Steps were not among the first six in the original draft. Bill W. incorporated them into the second draft so that there would be no further denying the absolute and demanding role that the God of one's understanding plays in the transformation process. Step Seven does not say when or how God will remove our shortcomings, only that we ask and recognize His continuous activity in our daily lives. These Steps further enhance the suggestion of Step Three.

I've given the term "transitional" to Steps Four though Nine. They are like rituals of initiation validating our acknowledgement of the problem and acceptance of the solution. They help get us started in the new life that we have chosen by discarding the past (Steps Four and Five) and strengthening us through God's help (Steps Six and Seven) to undertake the amends (Steps Eight and Nine) that we now see more clearly as a result of the self-examination that we have undertaken. Finally, the daily practice of Steps Ten, Eleven, and Twelve has remained constant throughout the whole transformation.

> *Step Ten:* Continued to take personal inventory and when we were wrong promptly admitted it.

> *Step Eleven:* Sought through prayer and meditation to improve our conscious contact with God *as we understood Him,* praying only for knowledge of His will for us and the power to carry that out.

> *Step Twelve:* Having had a spiritual awakening as the

result of these steps, we tried to carry this message to alcoholics, and to practice these principles in all our affairs.

The same pattern runs through the last three Steps, the daily exercises intended to keep us on the straight and narrow path. With Step Ten the emphasis is on self-knowledge through the personal inventory. Besides the acknowledgement of wrongs promptly admitted, this Step also invites us to a continual and conscious recognition of our strengths and weaknesses. *Twelve Steps and Twelve Traditions,* in elaborating on this Step, invites the recovering person to the practice of "spot checks," or checking on the origin and significance of inner movements of thoughts and feelings as they arise. This practice of "spot checks" allows us to be on top of our feelings before they take us by surprise and lead to inappropriate expressions of speech and behavior. They are particularly helpful in the development of personal integrity and the cultivation of honest relationships.

Adjacent to the inner circle is Step Twelve, prompting us to service, not only on behalf of other chemically dependent people, but in their absence to anyone in need who calls upon us to share our experience, strength, and hope. It is interesting that in piecing together what was to become the final version of Step Twelve, Bill W. initially wrote about encouraging the members to carry the message "to others, particularly alcoholics." Step Twelve gives meaning to one's life, subscribing as it does to the spiritual goal of purposeful lives. Having had a spiritual awakening, leading to a personality change spoken about in Appendix II of the Big Book, we seek to internalize the essential principle of the program: "I cannot do it by myself; I need others to help me," the "we" of the program.

Step Eleven draws the outer circumference and speaks to our relationship with the God of our understanding—a relationship that is cultivated through dialogue (prayer) and interior presence (meditation). Prayer and meditation are the daily practices essential to one's recovery. A refusal to pray derives from any number of reasons: no hope, no use, no God, no worth, no faith. We talk to ourselves and to others, but the God of our understanding gets shortchanged. It is important to remember that our God accepts us no matter where we are on our journey. To open the dialogue takes but a moment on our part. The prayers in the Big Book and *Twelve Steps and Twelve Traditions* are easily accessible and usually express what we would like to say. Thomas Merton's poetic prayer "The Road Ahead" and Francis Thompson's poem "The Hound of Heaven" stress God's eternal presence no matter what our dispositions or range of belief. God will continue to pursue us down the labyrinthine paths of our lives. Most everyone who has engaged in earnest and continuous prayer has experienced a rumor/stirring of angels, a mysterious and meaningful coincidence, an "aha" moment, or an unexpected confluence of unforeseen events.

The circles are symbolic of a never-ending process and ritualize both the power and the safety that a circle of relationships provides. This is a very simple program and at the same time a very profound program because it goes to the very heart of what makes us human/spiritual beings—our search for integrity, purpose, and meaning.

It is a simple program because it emphasizes what has been broken, namely our relationships. Moreover, just as there is no need to complicate the source of the problem, our powerlessness (Step One), similarly there is no need to complicate the solution, a power greater than ourselves (Steps Two and Three) and the spiritual exercises intended to assist us in living the solution (Steps Four through Twelve).

But, in truth, human beings do not like simple solutions. The more difficult and complicated they are, the stronger their appeal to our inflated egos that tell us that there is nothing that we cannot *fix* if we set our minds and wills to it. But chemical dependency cannot be *fixed*; the solution is *acceptance*. The longing for wholeness cannot be satisfied with chemicals but only with a God of our understanding, for our hearts are restless until they rest in God.

It is important that the reader understand why I have positioned the circles in the manner shown in diagram 5 (on page 27). The outer circles reflect our relationship with the God of our understanding. It is natural to question why this circle is not the second circle—the one next to the inmost circle or dot, representing the relationship with our inner and true self. The explanation is this. The arrangement of the circles ritualizes and serves as a reminder that the quality of our relationship with God is contingent/dependent upon the quality of our relationships with the company of our fellow human beings. Somewhere in the writings of John the Beloved, who is depicted as an eagle soaring to the very heart of his Higher Power, is the spiritual truth: "he who says he loves God and hates his neighbor is a liar and the truth is not in him."

In tracing the Steps in such a brief fashion there is the danger of sliding into a purely intellectual exercise and pushing aside their true purpose—that of transforming our lives. We can risk going through the motions if we are not consciously aware of the daily need to surrender, to internalize our exterior profession of powerlessness, the demand for a power greater than ourselves, and the practice of the spiritual exercises. Compliance, going through the motions, will not do it and its limitations will always catch up with us. It provides no serenity, no interior peace, and no spiritual comfort. What is true about life in general is true of the program in particular.

A word of caution: In the Big Book, the principles of recovery are the Twelve Steps and not the qualities or virtues that people cultivate on their spiritual journey. Thus, humility, honesty, patience, gratitude, respect, and so on are not the principles to which the Big Book, Bill W., or Dr. Bob were referring when they talked about the spiritual principles "to be practiced in all our affairs." These refer, most emphatically, to the Twelve Steps. We may associate or bond the virtue of humility or honesty or both with Step One or any of the other Steps, but the Twelve Steps do not favor any one virtue over the other.

The "God Issue"

When Bill W. submitted the Twelve Steps and the Big Book to the scrutiny of the New York and Akron groups, the radical left felt that God played too much of a role and that the word "God" should be deleted from the book entirely. On the other hand, some of the Christian-leaning members could not get enough of God. In his final editing, to please the atheist/agnostic wing, Bill described God as a "Power greater than ourselves" in Step Two. In Steps Three and Eleven he inserted the words "as we understood Him." And in Step Seven he deleted the words "on our knees." Moreover, he added that the Twelve Steps were to be "suggestions" only.

When people come through the door of Hazelden, the question about their religious orientation plays only a minuscule part in the whole assessment process, and there are no questions concerning one's personal belief in God. Each person is dispatched as soon as possible (after a twenty-four-hour stay on the skilled medical unit) to one of the units (to be their community for the next month) where that person is introduced to a group of fellow sufferers, not a group of believers.

There is a gradual orientation in subsequent days and weeks to Steps Two and Three. That is when feathers are ruffled by God talk, or fears and suspicions are alleviated by the same God talk. Some people are believers and have a deep personal faith in God; some are superficially inclined and going through a gallery of motions; still others are deeply hurt and angry at God/ religion. The agnostics and the atheists, in good or bad faith, are at the other end of the spectrum. Given this gamut of belief or disbelief, it is understandable that tolerance and respect need to be cultivated so that the community of sufferers can be formed for the first time and then gently nourished. "Most of us sense that real tolerance of other people's shortcomings and viewpoints and a respect for their opinions are attitudes which make us more useful to others. Our very lives as ex-problem drinkers, depend upon our constant thought of others and how we may help meet their needs" (*Alcoholics Anonymous,* pp. 19–20).

The dynamic is exactly what Dr. Bob said about Bill W. when they had their first in-depth conversation. It is hoped that during the early stages of treatment the patients cultivate a real tolerance for each other's shortcomings and a respect for their opinions (particularly their religious opinions). When it comes to chemical dependency then, the belief in God has to be accompanied by a belief that this God will be speaking to them through other recovering alcoholics just as Dr. Bob saw the God of his understanding speaking through Bill W. The exclusive belief in God will not do it for us. It has to be God and the Fellowship. For some, their Higher Power is simply the Fellowship. It's difficult to believe that Bill W. ever intended that the notion of a Higher Power be extended to include a stone or a doorknob.

Finally, there is much food for thought around the phrase "spiritual awakening" used in Step Twelve. How, what, where, when, and who? Appendix II of the Big Book beckons us to probe the richness of the phrase starting with the fact that initially Bill W. used the term "spiritual experience," which suggested a one-time happening (applicable to the beginning of his own recovery in the hospital through the "great white lights" occurrence), before settling on "spiritual awakening," which hints at ongoing insights and a gradual educational process rather than a one-time illumination. It is a personality change that others often see before the alcoholic himself is aware of it. Essential to this new way of thinking, which develops slowly, are the decline of the self-aggrandizing ego and the imposition of the common will of the "we" over the self will of the "I."

It may be oversimplistic, but one way of conceiving the personality change, or the spiritual awakening, is the gradual understanding and practice of the principle that "I cannot do it by myself; I need others to help me." The centrality of the "we" proposition is embedded deeply in the "kit of spiritual tools laid at our feet," namely the Steps. It includes Higher Power, God consciousness, or simply openness to spiritual principles, especially that of community: "Our journey through life is a community affair; someone has to say 'I will be with you.'"

No better way to end this chapter than the paragraph from the Big Book that comes immediately after the presentation of the Twelve Steps:

> *Many of us exclaimed, "What an order! I can't go through with it." Do not be discouraged. No one among us has been able to maintain anything like perfect adherence to these principles. We are not saints. The point is, that we are willing to grow along spiritual lines. The principles we have set down are guides to progress. We claim spiritual progress rather than spiritual perfection (p. 60).*

"Spirituality cannot be something a person toys with, a little compartment of their lives. It has to be at the core, in a way that affects every other part of their lives."

STEPHEN COVEY

CHAPTER 4

Benchmarks for Spiritual Growth

"Our stories disclose in a general way what we used to be like, what happened, and what we are like now." (*Alcoholics Anonymous,* p. 58) The phrases "what we used to be like" and "what we are like now" imply the idea of growth or movement, the transition from one phase of life to another. This leads to the inevitable question of whether we can uncover benchmarks that would help in assessing and marking that growth, even if it is, the spiritual and not strictly scientific or empirical realm. Indeed it does throw people off balance when asked in a conference how they would measure their spiritual growth. Part of the reason is that they have a hard time coming to grips with the word "spiritual," and the other part is that they wonder how the spiritual (as invisible, or ghostly) can really be scientifically or empirically measured. They have never truly thought of identifying the truly spiritual with the truly human (in its relational dimension) and vice versa.

The Big Book, Appendix II, states that quite often our friends can see the signs of our spiritual awakening, our personality change, long before we ourselves are conscious of it. This reinforces the value of sponsorship and participation in the Fellowship so that others can point out to us the clear signs of our spiritual fitness/growth (or as is sometimes the case, our spiritual retrogression).

One of the clearest measurements of spiritual growth is the practice of Steps Ten, Eleven, and Twelve. It is the punctual and daily routine of personal inventory, prayer and meditation, and sharing (carrying the message). Going to meetings; talking with a sponsor; reading the Big Book; and adding to the days, months, years, and anniversaries of abstaining from chemicals are all marks that at least quantify our spiritual growth. The internal mark is the practice of these spiritual principles (the Twelve Steps) in all our affairs.

Moving from isolation to the cultivation of good, healthy relationships with self, others, and the God of our understanding is another spiritual benchmark. Releasing our true self from the solitary confinement to which our addictive self has confined it frees us to return to the land of the living from the land of objects. This freedom, in turn, allows us to nurture former or new relationships with family members and friends who love us for who we truly are. Moreover, this new freedom allows us to reach a more comfortable place with the God of our understanding whose love is unconditional and who reaches out to us wherever we are in our journey.

> Having once escaped from the addictive self, there is a danger that we can very easily allow other demons in, or will allow the roles that we play (such as doctor, priest, professor, nurse, and so on) to take charge and once again remand the real self to the dungeon from which it has just recently been liberated.

> It took Rachel a long time after her treatment to understand that her recovery was not wrapped up in her profession as a "clean" nurse and confined to the safety, comfort, and *isolation* afforded by her condominium. It required some time to translate the principles of community, of the "we" of the program, to her life after treatment. Fortunately, she connected with a sponsor who insisted that she socialize after meetings and then eventually with other people outside the Fellowship. She took a major, and initially a somewhat terrifying, step when she joined a women's golf league for beginners. Soon the "Ya Ya Sisterhood" was not a book that she read but another group of likeminded women who found the company of one another intoxicating, but without the chemicals.

The validity of this measurement for spiritual growth can always be tested by those closest to us whose scrutiny we can welcome with unfailing trust. We simply have to ask them what our behavior is revealing to them.

In a little inspirational pamphlet entitled *Toward Spirituality*, Jerry

Dollard, the first director of Hazelden's Renewal Center, sees the beginning of spiritual growth in a passage from page 84 of the Big Book, which he has summarized here: "Having entered the world of the spirit . . . we continue to watch for selfishness, dishonesty, resentments, and fear." He classifies these four qualities as negative spirituality. He then contrast them with four other qualities that serve as the foundation for positive spirituality. Combined with the negative indicators, they qualify as valid markers for spiritual transformation. Thus spiritual growth moves from:

Dishonesty	to	Honesty
Fear	to	Trust
Self-centeredness	to	Acceptance
Resentments	to	Gratitude

Scrutinizing one or all of these shortcomings on a daily basis and noting our progress in a journal can be a reliable gauge of spiritual progress.

The same journal can be an instrument for recording daily insights in our internal growth in honesty, open-mindedness, and willingness, emphasized as indispensable in Appendix II of the Big Book. One cannot emphasize enough the importance of a journal, written in regularly, as an exercise for sensing and capturing our internal growth in these spiritual/human qualities. Our reliance is upon the proposition (paraphrased from Thomas Merton) that "to be truly human is to be truly spiritual, and to be truly spiritual is to be truly human."

Similar to what has been outlined above regarding negative and positive spirituality is another method of measuring spiritual growth. Referred to as the "bedevilments" by the Big Book (p. 52) is a list of negative qualities that thoroughly describe what it was like before. Contrasted with the widely known "promises" of the Big Book (pp. 83–84), pointing to what it is like now, together they provide a singular checklist for spiritual growth. Consistent reflections captured in a journal can serve as a barometer, displaying our progress, mediocrity, or inertia—a barometer sensitive to the fluctuations that are part and parcel of our living one day at a time. The following abbreviated checklist might serve as a simple inventory:

What It Was Like Before	*What It Is Like Now*
Bedevilments	*Promises*
Trouble with personal relationships	Fear of people leaves us
Could not control our emotional natures	Self-pity and self-seeking slips away
Prey to misery and depression	Our whole attitude on life changes
Could not make a living	Economic insecurity leaves us
Feelings of uselessness	Feelings of uselessness disappear
We were unhappy	We intuitively know how to handle situations that used to baffle us

The clearest benchmark, of course, is that "we will comprehend the word serenity and we will know peace." This is the one that I personally prefer above all. It is truly God's gift and manifests itself externally in the acceptance prayer on page 417 of the Big Book, which contains one of the most inspirational passages in AA literature: "Unless I accept life completely on life's terms, I cannot be happy."

The final benchmark I would suggest—probably the most important of all—may be the most difficult to describe. Even the dictionary has a hard time defining *humility*, inasmuch as it describes this quality by what it is not (for example, it is not characterized by arrogance or grandiosity). Etymologically it derives from the Latin word *humus*, which means ground or earth. According to the Torah, when God created man he formed him from the earth and then breathed His Spirit into him, thus giving him life. In this sense, humility means the acceptance of one's dependence upon a God of one's understanding and the acceptance of a role of equality (neither superiority nor inferiority) with the rest of creation (the rest of the earth, the *humus*). In Jewish writings, the holy man is described as one practicing justice and mercy and one "walking *humbly* with God." As such it serves as the foundation of all the Steps that requires the acceptance of the "we" principle that "I cannot do it by myself; I need others to help me."

Guilt and Shame

It may not be clear at first, but one of the measurements of our growth or retrogression is how we handle guilt and shame. We can let these feelings overwhelm us or we can examine the role they play in our lives in general and in the life of the chemically dependent person in particular, and after understanding their role, accept it and move on. One of the implications of freeing our real self from the dungeon of dependency, the keys to which were held by the addictive self, is: "How do we unlock the lingering shackles of guilt and shame?" The following is my personal slant on the subject.

I am sure that there are some exceptions, but we belong to a species in which every member has had an initial experience of *guilt* (derived from doing something inappropriate that is not in accordance with his or her value system) or of *shame* (I am a bad person. How could *I* do that? What will people think of me?), both rooted in self-esteem or the lack thereof. One of the greatest obstacles to recovery is the feeling of guilt or shame resulting from inappropriate behavior under the influence of alcohol or drugs or both. While the explanation that this behavior was the result of the disease/illness might be somewhat theoretically satisfying for the addicted person, it will not wash in its attempt to remove what he feels is his responsibility for his reprehensible behavior, even when he is reminded that he is not a bad person, but a good person with a bad disease.

Guilt and shame come with the price of being imperfect human beings. They usually make their appearance together, and since the feelings accompanying both are usually the same, they are difficult to differentiate. Guilt is about what we do (behavior), about mistakes, about what we have done wrong. Our behavior/conduct triggers unpleasant feelings. Shame triggers unpleasant feelings about who we are, our very selves. It insists that we are bad people, whereas guilt, as we have indicated, speaks to our inappropriate behavior.

Shame strikes at our self-esteem. It is unhealthy since it subtly demands that we be perfect. Guilt can be healthy, reminding us of the demands upon our own relationship with the God of our understanding, others, and ourselves. It is my belief that even shame has some value in that it reminds us that in this life all of us fall short of the mark, that we are imperfect human beings, and that we need not meet the expectations of others, but only those of the God of our understanding.

Shame and guilt are serious blocks to recovery because they fill the chemically dependent person with a sense of hopelessness and despair when she is faced with the consequences of her drinking and using. That chemical dependency is an illness affords little balm for the feelings arising from the serious unmanageability that her using has caused.

There is, however, another way of looking at this picture. The following poem by Edward Sanford Martin entitled "My Name Is Legion" highlights a condition common to all of us:

Within my earthly temple there's a crowd,
There's one of us that's humble, one that's proud.
There's one that brokenhearted for his sins,
There's one that unrepentant sits and grins.
There's one that loves his neighbor as himself,
And one that cares for naught but fame and pelf;
From much corroding care I should be free,
If I could once determine, which is me?

This passage describes a struggle that has played a prominent role in the history of Western thought and spirituality. Poets, writers, religious thinkers, psychologists—people from all fields—have all sought to explain the origins of this dualism, its personal drama and outcomes. Paul of Tarsus (the great Christian missionary) witnessed for many when he exclaimed: "I do not do what I want to—and what I do I detest. Miserable man that I am. Who will save me from the body of this death?" (Romans 7:24)

Almost two thousand years later, Carl Jung, the famous Swiss psychiatrist, was commenting on the same enigma: "What drives people to war with themselves is the intuition or knowledge that they consist of two people in opposition to one another. The conflict may be between the sensual and spiritual man, or between the ego and the shadow. It is what Faust means when he says: 'Two souls, alas, dwell within my breast apart'" (p. 173).

Indeed all of us are called to struggle with this duality within us and to live with that inherent tension, consciously, honestly, and with courage. In previous pages I have pointed out how the chemically dependent struggle with that tension between the two selves and how the addictive personality emerges from the false self and eventually dominates that self who it truly is. The addictive self is like a boa constrictor slowly squeezing the life out of the real self. Consequently, it is important to recognize that the addictive self is really the exhibitionist responsible for the addict's unmanageability and patterns of self-defeating behavior. It is to the addictive self that the guilt and shame must be attributed. The real self has lost its identity, confined as it is to the deep dungeon where its cries are like echoes returning without notice.

Raphael was unable to remember the exact number of detox units and treatment settings that he had been through. He knew that they were many. What he did remember and what he was fully conscious of was the burden of guilt and shame that he carried, which grew heavier at each station at which he rested along the way. His losses were severe and continued to pile up: divorced from his wife, loss of job after job despite his many talents, loss of dreams and physical and mental health. Worst of all, his four children no longer communicated with him. During his first month at Hazelden, his whole demeanor spoke of hopelessness. He walked about the unit with his head down, uncommunicative despite the best efforts of his peers.

Two things eventually helped to bring him out of his shell. First, he was given the assignment by his counselor to approach one peer each day and ask that peer to share with him one positive quality that the peer saw in him. After 28 days he had 28 positive comments. As he continued to work on his sections on powerlessness, he finally began to understand that he was powerless over his behavior while he was drinking and using. Second, he was asked to repeat as his affirmation before groups and community meetings the phrase: "It really wasn't I who did that" with the emphasis on the pronoun "I" so that he would come to understand that if he hadn't been under the influence of chemicals, his real self would never have acted that way. This helped to take a little of the edge off his guilt and shame.

Part of the problem was that Raphael was a deeply religious man, a Catholic by birth, education, and tradition, whose conscience and code took him down a tunnel in which he could easily get lost. He had to reflect upon the unconditional forgiveness of his God. Accepting that, he gradually came to see that he had to forgive himself. Otherwise he would be making himself better than God.

It took him a long time but before he left Hazelden for a halfway house he was walking about with his head up, talking with his peers, and dealing in a healthy fashion with his guilt and shame. Best of all, he had a visit from two of his children two weeks before he departed. His spirit was finally discovering the peace and rest that had eluded him for so many years.

Thus there are grounds for overturning the sentence of guilt. One must not be too quick to brush aside the anguish of the chemically dependent that "I cannot believe that I did that." The claim that the wrong person is being prosecuted deserves a hearing. The real culprit, our slick demon, needs to stand in the dock and accept the censure of guilty. Some may see casuistry or sophistry in all of this, but I stand by my belief that we are all made up of two selves in conflict with one another. Having said all of this, I know that feelings of guilt and shame will continue to rise to the surface. I simply urge that they be located where they truly belong—on the head of the addictive self. Every addict should take comfort in the knowledge and realization that this unmanageable behavior "is not who I truly am."

Where does an addict stand in the sight of the God of her understanding? Forgiveness comes seventy times seven (in other words, infinitely). All she has to do is ask for it, pick herself up, and move forward as her journey unfolds, no matter how many times she may stumble.

"The most beautiful thing we can experience is the mysterious."

ALBERT EINSTEIN

CONCLUSION

The Cultivation of the Interior Life

What then is spirituality? On the one hand the word serves as a "catchall" for a sanitized, feel-good, boutique, therapeutic spirituality that makes no demands, calls for no sacrifice, asks for no conversion, but only soothes and affirms. It is a "glow word" defying definition except that its use makes us feel better, either individually or communally. On the other hand, for many it does have a precise negative connotation. It is *not* religion, although it may have some connection with religion. Describing that connection is left to the theologian whose task it is to deal with the esoteric and the mysterious. It's simply more popular to be spiritual and rather old-fashioned to be religious.

Without being drawn too much farther afield, allow me a few personal observations that may serve the needs of recovering people (whose experience with religion has been of the negative sort) as they begin or continue on their recovering journey of ascent into greater awareness "of their essential selves, beyond ego and personal desires" (Arrien, p. 13). For some the word "spiritual" conveys the sense of something ghostly, something invisible. As such it appeals to people who believe in the power of the invisible world.

However, there is another way of understanding and accepting the word. Spirit has to do with life, with life-giving, with the very air we breathe. There are numerous words in the English language with "spirit" as their root and which convey this very idea of life. "E*spire*" means to stop breathing and with that stoppage the spirit goes out of us. A "re*spira*tor" is a machine that keeps us breathing so that the spirit will remain within us. To "a*spira*te" is to remove something that has stopped our breathing so that we can breathe normally again. Analogously, to "in*spire*" is to breathe some life or vitality into someone to desire/achieve a higher goal or purpose.

Spirit in these examples has to do with breathing, so that if a person stops breathing, the spirit is no longer present. And according to the descendents of Abraham, it all started when God fashioned man from a handful of earth and breathed into his nostrils the breath of life so that man became a living soul.

For centuries in the Western world, spirituality meant the cultivation of this life-giving principle/spirit by means of a set of exercises (asceticism) intended for that purpose, essential to which were prayer and meditation. It is this spirit that affords us the power to seek out the invisible presence, the mystery (or as I, along with others, like to describe it, the "cloud of the unknowing") through the visible signs that manifest themselves in a variety of ways throughout the universe and the world in which we live. It is this principle that serves as the compass that directs us to what is congruent behavior in the pursuit of the good, the true, and the beautiful. It is this spirit, finally, that nourishes our relationships with God, others, and ourselves. Spirituality cannot be something that simply makes me feel good without any reference to another. It has to be relational. Spirituality is more than a "glow word," a "catchall," and a "feel-good"; it is not simply an end in itself, though many people think that way in our modern world. Indeed, spirituality is the art and practice of nurturing that life-giving, seminal principle in all of us that allows us to discover our real selves (who we truly are) and to relate to others, the universe, and the God of our understanding—simply intended, to capture the abiding spirit in all. Stated in another way, it is the art and practice of cultivating our interior lives through all the Steps but especially through prayer and meditation (the Eleventh Step). French philosopher and paleontologist Pierre Teilhard de Chardin has been quoted as saying: "We are not human beings having a spiritual experience. We are spiritual beings having a human experience."

Many times I have patients who are returning to treatment a second, third, or even more times say to me that the reason that they did not remain sober is that they did not get the spirituality of the program. By that phrase they usually mean one of three things: (1) they haven't continued with the protocol of steps and community; (2) they are still stuck on the God issue (in many instances this is simply a smoke screen); or (3) they cannot "get" the Third Step. It's easy to respond that they have not practiced "these principles [the Twelve Steps] in all their affairs" or they have not lived in fellowship with other recovering people. True, that is the protocol for recovery. But is this all that spirituality is about? As I was writing the preceding pages and drawing the charts, the question kept nagging at me: What is missing? Understanding the Steps and working the Steps is indeed important. But that does not cut to the heart of the matter. In truth we have to go one level deeper to capture the spiritual life and in turn a life of sobriety and serenity. It is not simply enough to be called to a change of mind, a way of thinking, and a way of acting. What is demanded is a change of heart. The phrases that best capture this are: "take it to heart" and "put your heart and soul into it." I sense that is what people mean when they assert that they have not "gotten the spirituality of the program." It is not about jousting with the God issue, but rather about cultivating the interior life to bring about a change of heart that encourages total acceptance.

In previous pages dealing with Step Three, I wrote that "making a decision" to choose recovery requires that we "act accordingly" using the recovery capital that has been freely provided us, such as meetings, the Steps, and so on. This working capital, however, to be truly effective has to be grounded in humility and gratitude, and sustained by the habits of prayer and meditation so that we experience our recovery as coming truly from within and not simply externally repetitive and spiritually deprived.

I believe that we make a serious mistake when we contrapose rather than juxtapose spirituality and religion. The *heart* of religion in the Western world as found in both Jewish and

Christian texts is loving God with one's whole heart and one's neighbor as one's self. And the *core* (heart) of its practice is the care for the poor, the elderly, the widow, the orphan, and the stranger. It's difficult to understand how the spiritual person could argue with any of those demands. I suspect that the religious core (the *heart* of the matter)—love and action—apply equally to what it means to be a spiritual person and what it means to be a religious person. Of course, if the purpose of the spiritual is to eliminate the participation of God in the equation then there is no basis for forming an alliance between the two.

Indeed, for many people, their antagonism is directed not so much toward the basic tenets of religion as outlined above (in other words, love and its practice), but toward the self-centered denominationalism into which religion has fractured, the claims for absolute truth, and the intolerance and self-righteousness inherent in much of that denominationalism.

Diagram 6 suggests how religion and spirituality can be viewed as similar or dissimilar. The questions proposed are from the book *How Then, Shall We Live?* by Wayne Muller.

Chemicals strip us of meaning and purpose, rob us of whatever legacy we might wish to bequeath to the communities to which we are linked, and strip us of any possibility of making a difference. My fundamental belief is that if we are truly spiritual persons, or striving to be such, then we really have to pause in life's journey and ponder the questions: Who am I? Am I making a difference? How shall I define my legacy? And how shall I live? We need to answer them as best we know how and allow them to serve as the foundation for lives of integrity. Again: "Do this and you shall live." There is obviously congruence between the questions on the right side of the above diagram and the answers on the left side. Life can be very dull if we don't ask questions. Life can be even more dull if at some point in our journey we believe we have all the answers. Rainer Maria Rilke, in his *Letters to a Young Poet,* has a beautiful reminder

DIAGRAM 6

Religion and/or Spirituality

A way of life that is . . .

A GIVEN	A SEARCH

Provides Answers

- Meaning and Purpose
- Code of Conduct
- Creed of Beliefs
- Rituals of Worship

Poses Questions

- Who Am I?
- How Shall I Live?
- What Is My Legacy?
- Am I Making a Difference?

God is a Given   God is Suggested

to live in the questions that are in our hearts, and not to be concerned about the answers. It is much more poetic than to suggest that we need to live in the "belly of the whale" at turning points in our lives. But they both carry the same message.

Paul Tillich's thought is the pebble in our shoe that our knowledge of God is so infinitesimally small and inadequate. God does not change, but our perceptions of God do, and hopefully for the better, the wiser. I have paraphrased his words as applicable to myself: "I believed in God when I was 17; and I continued to believe in God when I turned 77; but clearly it was not the same God."

It was no wonder that Michael relapsed not long after he left treatment. He seemed to have gotten the part about his powerlessness, the recognition that he could not drink anymore, and he seemed fully prepared to act on that knowledge. But he did not embrace change very well and did pretty much as he pleased when it came to the unit expectations and participating as a member of the community. He felt that if he did not drink he would do much better in the business world to which he returned, indeed clear headed but not clean hearted. He soon relapsed into his unsavory business practices, forgetting that honesty was the heart and soul of his program.

He was much too busy to practice the daily prayers that he had learned in treatment, especially the Peace Prayer of St. Francis. He lost the practice of "spot checks," which at least initially had turned him away from shady deals. The amends that he intended to practice were quickly forgotten, rather buried with his preoccupation with "more pressing matters." The relapse took place long before he took his first drink, his second, and his third. Michael did not understand that abstinence alone does not in any way make us spiritually fit. Fortunately, he found enough humility to listen to his sponsor and return to treatment.

Recovery for addicted people begins the moment they splinter the beam of their denial and begin to understand the life-threatening nature of their illness. This encounter with one's mortality is ultimately spiritual as it archetypically involves a death/rising process—a dying of the addicted self and a rising of the real self.

Carl Jung, in a letter to Bill W., suggested that "alcoholism is a spiritual disease at the bottom of which is man's yearning for wholeness." People search for meaning/wholeness in their lives and discover it in different places: power, pleasure, wealth, or chemicals. Jung, Viktor Frankl, and Paul Tillich all focused upon what has become widely recognized as the problem for individuals today: the problem of meaning and its opposite (meaninglessness). In traditional language it has been a religious problem. We can call it a spiritual one, since the anxiety deriving from a life without meaning arises from the loss of a spiritual center, "from the need for an answer, however symbolic and indirect, to the question of the meaning of existence" (Tillich, pp. 139–140).

Some people look for an answer in drugs, others in alcohol, and still others in both. As Bill W. wrote: "More than most people, I think, alcoholics want to know who they are, what life is all about, whether they have a divine origin, an appointed destiny, and whether there is a system of cosmic justice and love" (*As Bill Sees It,* p. 323). But they have difficulty "living life on life's terms."

Returning to the metaphor of journey, the major difficulty for those addicted to chemicals is that they seek to bypass or leap over the challenges that life demands of all of us, to become whole, not through struggle and self-examination; and especially not through the crucible of pain. Life's journey is full of crises (those encounters with our mortality) that must be dealt with in a constructive manner. It is in this sense that chemical dependency is but a symptom of the most comprehensive *dis-ease* (discomfort), namely, humankind's search for self, for meaning, for wholeness.

It is in this context that Bill W. proposed the Fellowship and composed the Twelve Steps, both as the remedy for the disease of alcoholism. With community we are given love and support, the Big Book maps out the healing journey, and the Twelve Steps provide a set of spiritual exercises to accompany us on our spiritual odyssey, all providing strength and courage for those critical moments (crises) that are bound to occur throughout life's journey. Like spring melt waters cascading through a canyon, the community and the Twelve Steps unleash a tremendous healing power. For who on this planet does not feel the need for healing, for dealing with that incompleteness, that lack of wholeness, that vulnerability deep within us—a shadow from which we would like to escape but which lurks behind us no matter which way we turn?

References

Alcoholics Anonymous. 4th ed. New York: Alcoholics Anonymous World Services, 2001.

Arrien, Angeles. *The Second Half of Life.* Boulder, CO: Sounds True, 2005.

Dollard, Jerry. *Toward Spirituality.* Center City, MN: Hazelden, 1983.

Hilton, Dave. "Global Health and the Limits of Medicine." *Second Opinion* (January 1993).

Jung, Carl. *Modern Man in Search of a Soul.* New York: Harcourt, Brace & Company, 1933.

Lopez, Barry. *Crow and Weasel.* San Francisco, CA: North Point Press, 1900.

Marin, Edward Sanford, "My Name Is Legion," in *Masterpieces of Religious Verse,* ed. James Dalton Morrison. New York: Harper, 1948: 274.

Merton, Thomas. *Thoughts in Solitude.* New York: Farrar, Straus and Giroux, 1958.

Nakken, Craig. *The Addictive Personality: Understanding the Addictive Process and Compulsive Behavior.* 2nd edition. Center City, MN: Hazelden, 1996.

Thompson, Francis. *The Hound of Heaven and Other Poems.* Wellesley, MA: Branden Books, 1978.

Tillich, Paul. *The Courage to Be.* New Haven, CT: Yale University Press, 1952.

Twelve Steps and Twelve Traditions. New York: Alcoholics Anonymous World Services, 1952.

W., Bill. *As Bill Sees It: the A.A. Way of Life: Selected Writings of A.A.'s Co-founder.* New York: Alcoholics Anonymous World Services, 1967.

About the Author

When Damian McElrath arrived at Hazelden in 1977 as a clinical pastoral trainee, he was struck by the power that Hazelden had for radically changing the course of people's lives.

Over the course of the next three decades at Hazelden, he engaged in a variety of administrative roles, the last of which was executive vice president of recovery services. Following his retirement in 1995, he authored a book containing Hazelden's complete history and biographies of Pat Butler and Dan Anderson, two of Hazelden's key figures. Throughout this time he continued to reflect upon that capacity to bring about change through the spiritual program of AA.

Returning to Jellinek as a chaplain in 2003 provided him the opportunity to reflect more seriously on how it works. That is the genesis of this volume and the completion of his dream to put in writing the power that Hazelden has and to which it must be faithful if it is to provide the milieu for change—and change is what recovery is all about.

Before coming to Hazelden, Damian spent three decades as a Franciscan priest serving the spiritual needs of others in a variety of roles, including teaching, counseling, and administrative work. He was president of St. Bonaventure University from 1972 to 1976. He has published a number of scholarly books and articles on historical and theological topics.